READING/WRITING COMPANION

Mc
Graw
Hill
Education

Cover: Nathan Love, Erwin Madrid

mheducation.com/prek-12

Send all inquiries to:
McGraw-Hill Education
Two Penn Plaza
New York, NY 10121

ISBN: 978-0-07-901801-4
MHID: 0-07-901801-7

Printed in the United States of America.

11 LMN 23

D

Welcome to Wonders!

Read exciting **Literature**, **Science**, and **Social Studies** texts!

 LEARN about the world around you!

 THINK, **SPEAK**, and **WRITE** about genres!

 COLLABORATE in discussions and inquiry!

 EXPRESS yourself!

my.mheducation.com

Use your student login to read texts and practice phonics, spelling, grammar, and more!

Unit 5 Figure It Out

The Big Idea

Week 1 • See It, Sort It

Digital Tools Find this eBook and other resources at: **my.mheducation.com**

Week 2 • Up in the Sky

Week 3 • Great Inventions

Week 4 • Sounds All Around

Week 5 • Build It!

Handout/Getty Images Entertainment/Getty Images

Writing and Grammar

Wrap Up the Unit

Figure It Out

Listen to and think about the poem "Jack Frost."

 Talk about what designs or shapes you see on the window in the photo.

The
Big Idea

How can we make sense of the world around us?

Talk About It

Essential Question How can we classify and categorize things?

Talk about how this girl is sorting things. Use words that name the kinds of items she is sorting.

Write three ways to sort things.

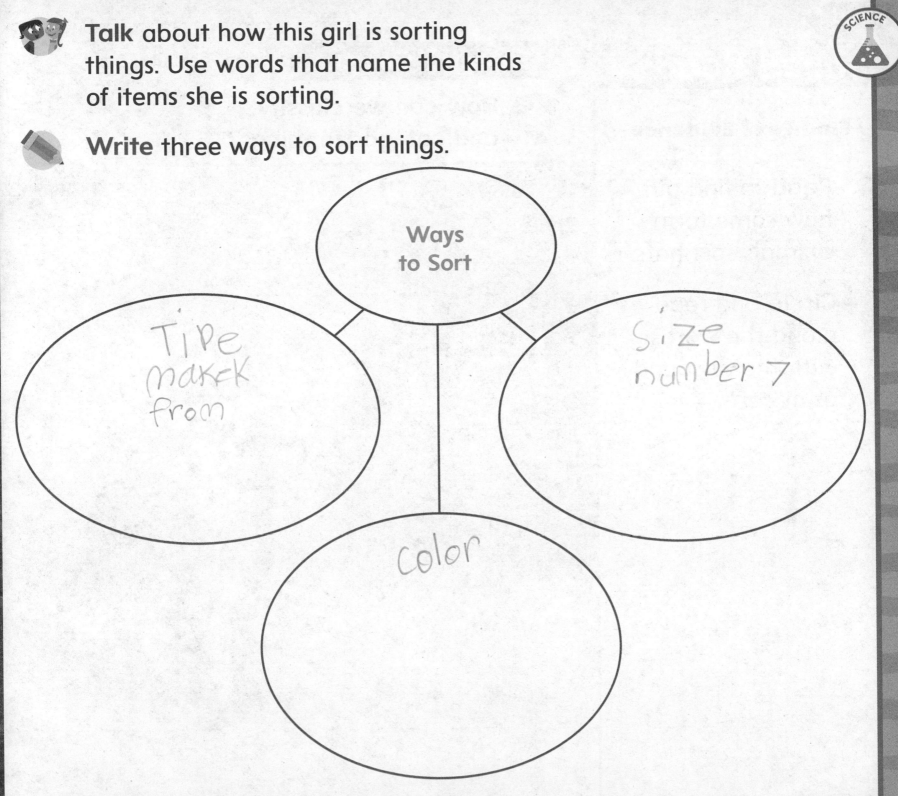

Ways to Sort

TiPe makek from

Size number 7

Color

Find Text Evidence

 Read to find out how some farm animals sort hats.

Circle and read aloud the words with the *ar* sound as in *cart*.

Essential Question

? How can we classify and categorize things?

Clark's Farm

A Barn Full of Hats

yarn

Find Text Evidence

Circle and read aloud each word with the *ar* sound as in *cart*.

Underline and read aloud the word *four*.

One day, four farm animals found a box in the barn. They opened it up.

What was inside? Hats, hats, and more hats!

"Look at all those hats! Who wants one?" asked Hen.

"I do!" cried Horse. "It's smart to wear a hat. A hat will keep the sun out of my eyes."

Find Text Evidence

Underline and read aloud the words *round* and *put*.

Think about the story so far. Make a prediction about who will want the next hat.

Hen stuck her head in the box. She pulled out a flat, round hat. "Try this hat," Hen told Horse.

"No, that hat is too flat," said Horse.

"A flat hat makes a good nest!" clucked Hen. So she took the hat and she marched away.

Pig pushed his head in the box. He pulled out a bright red hat. "Put on this hat," Pig told Horse.

"No, that hat is too red," said Horse.

"A red hat looks fine!" grunted Pig. So he put on the hat and he marched away.

 Find Text Evidence

Talk about Horse. What have you learned about him so far?

Talk about the prediction you made about the next hat. Do you need to correct it?

Cat poked her head in the box. She pulled out a thick yarn hat. "Try this hat!" Cat told Horse.

"No, that hat is too thick," said Horse.

"Thick yarn is nice," said Cat. "I will take the **whole** hat apart, so I can play with the yarn." She dragged the hat away.

"So many hats, but none for me!" sighed Horse.

Shared Read

Find Text Evidence

Retell the events in order.

Focus on Fluency

Take turns reading aloud to a partner.

- Read each word carefully.

- Read so it sounds like speech.

Just then, Farmer Clark came into the barn. His hat was large and floppy.

"If only I had that hat!" said Horse. "That hat will shade my eyes!"

Horse grabbed the hat in his teeth!

Farmer Clark laughed. He put the hat on Horse. It stayed on with no **trouble**. "It fits well," Farmer Clark said.

Horse trotted to the barnyard. Clip, clop! He held his head high. "Yes, this is the hat for me!" said Horse.

Vocabulary

 Listen to the sentences and look at the photos.

 Talk about the words.

Write your own sentences using each word.

trouble

A goat can get into **trouble**.

I o

whole

The **whole** barn is painted red.

Multiple Meanings

To figure out which meaning of a word is used, think about the other words in the story.

🔍 Find Text Evidence

I know that *cried* has more than one meaning. The words *"I do!"* tell me Horse is excited. I think *cried* in this story means "yelled out with excitement."

"I do!" cried Horse.

Your Turn

What words help you figure out the meaning of *bright* on page 17?

A **fantasy** is a made-up story that could not really happen. It often has animal characters who act like people, and dialogue, or words that the characters say.

 Reread the dialogue in the story.

 Talk about what you learn about Horse from what he says.

Choose two characters from the story. Write what you learn about them from what they say.

Characters	What I Learn About Them

Point of view is the way that a story character thinks or feels. What a character says and does helps you understand his or her point of view.

 Reread "A Barn Full of Hats."

 Talk about what the characters say and do.

 Write clues from the dialogue that show the characters' points of view.

Character	Clue	Point of View

Retell the story using the illustrations and words from the story.

Write about the story. Use text evidence.

Why is the first button Frog finds not the right button?

_____

- -

_____

_____

- -

_____

Text Evidence

Page

What really happened to Toad's button?

- -

_____

_____

- -

_____

Text Evidence

Page

Talk about how the stories are the same and different. Speak in complete sentences.

Write about the stories.

How are the characters Horse and Toad the same?

_____

- -

_____

- -

_____

What does *A Lost Button* teach about friendship?

_____

- -

_____

_____

- -

_____

Combine Information

As you read, *A Lost Button*, think about how your ideas about friends change.

First, I thought . . .

Then I thought . . .

Talk about what is happening in the story on page 144.

Write three things Frog says that show he is a good friend.

How does the author show that Frog is a good friend? Share your answer.

_____

- -

_____

- -

_____

Talk about how Toad acts when someone shows him a button on pages 148–149.

 Write three clues that show Toad's feelings.

How does the author show Toad's feelings?
Share your answer.

_____

- -

_____

- -

_____

Talk about what Toad says on page 151.

Write clues from the text and illustration that tell you how Toad feels about Frog.

Text	Illustrations

How does the author help you understand how Toad is a good friend? Share your answer.

_____

_____

_____

_____

Write About It

Do you think that Frog or Toad is the better friend? Why?

SCIENCE

Sort It Out

Some things are alike. Some are different. We can sort things by looking at what is the same about them. We can sort them by their size, shape, and color.

Find the buttons in this picture. Let's sort them!

 Read the title and look at the picture. Make a prediction about the text.

 Underline the sentence that tells how to sort things.

 Talk about how the picture helps you understand how to sort.

How many round buttons can you see? How many square buttons can you see? What other shapes do you see? Add up the number of red buttons. Are there more red or yellow buttons? Can you find buttons with four holes? How else could you sort these buttons?

 Talk about the picture and text. Do you need to change your prediction?

 Circle the words the author uses to describe the buttons.

 Talk about other ways you can sort.

Quick Tip

Use the questions in the text for ideas about how to sort.

Talk about the questions in the text.
Where do you find the answers?

 Write the answers to the last three
questions the author asks on page 34.

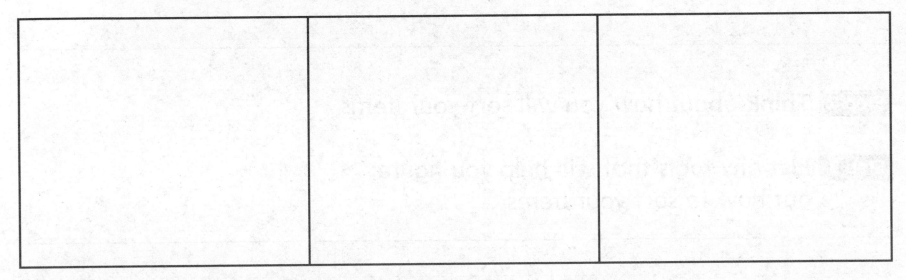

Why did the author include questions in
the text? Share your answer.

_____

_____

_____

_____

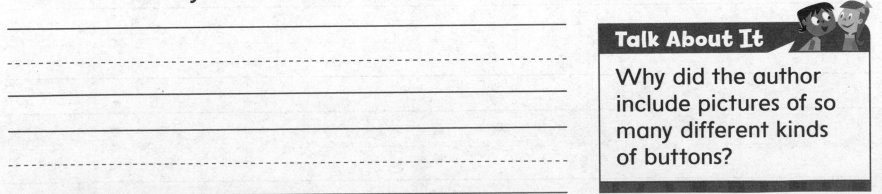

Talk About It

Why did the author
include pictures of so
many different kinds
of buttons?

My Collection

Step 1 **Choose** some items to collect and sort.
Write what you will collect.

_____

- -

_____

Step 2 **Think** about how you will sort your items.

Step 3 **List** any tools that will help you figure
out how to sort your items.

_____

- -

_____

- -

_____

- -

_____

Step 4 Collect your items. Then use your tools to sort and tally your items.

Type	Number

Step 5 Write what you learned.

_____

- -

_____

- -

_____

- -

_____

- -

_____

- -

_____

Step 6 Choose how to present your work.

Circle the items the ship is carrying. Then circle what the ship is made of.

 Compare how the items in the poem and the buttons in "Sort It Out" can be sorted.

Ye Fairy Ship

A ship, a ship a-sailing,
A-sailing on the sea,
And it was deeply laden
With pretty things for me;
There were raisins in the cabin,
And almonds in the hold;
The sails were made of satin,
And the mast it was of gold.

— by Walter Crane

What I Know Now

Think about the texts you heard and read this week about sorting. Write what you learned.

_____

- -

_____

- -

_____

- -

_____

 Think about what else you would like to learn about sorting. Talk about your ideas.

 Share one thing you learned this week about fantasy stories.

Essential Question What can you see in the sky?

Talk and ask questions about what this girl sees in the night sky.

Write what you see in the sky.

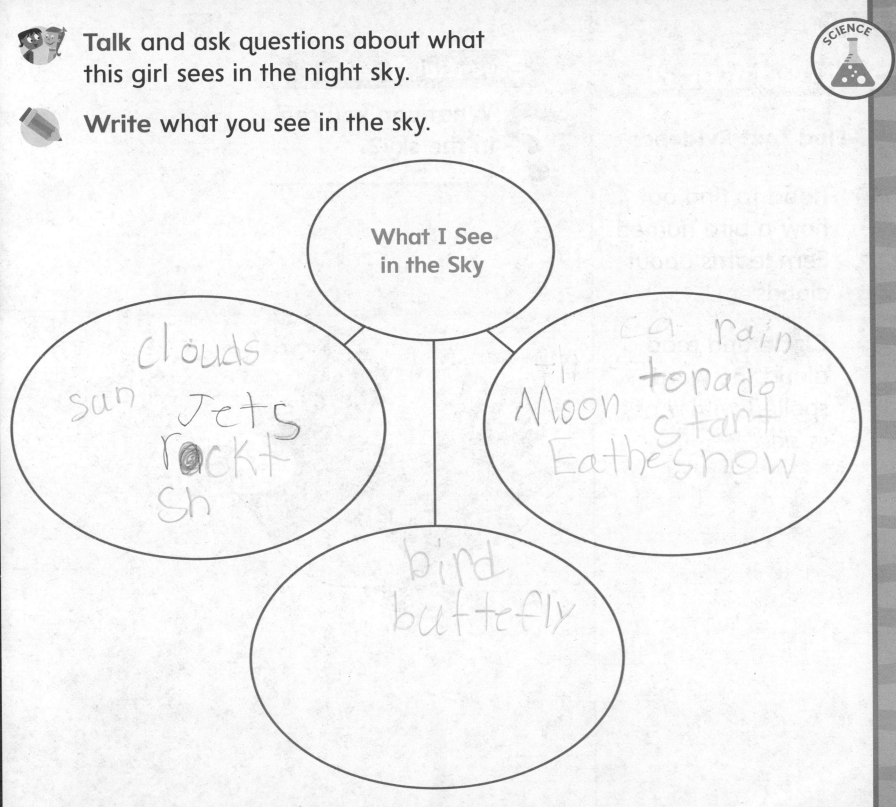

What I See in the Sky

clouds
sun Jets
rackt
Sh

ca rain
Moon tonado
start
Eatheshow

bird
buttefly

(bkgd)StockTrek/Photodisc/Getty Images; (r)Image Source/Getty Images

Shared Read

Find Text Evidence

 Read to find out how a bird named Fern learns about clouds.

Circle and read aloud the word spelled with *ir* as in *skirt*.

Essential Question

What can you see in the sky?

A Bird Named Fern

Shared Read

 Find Text Evidence

Circle and read aloud the word spelled with *or* as in *worm*.

Make a prediction about what Fern will do next.

Little Fern was always full of questions! She wanted to know about everything in the world.

One day, Fern saw something up in the sky.

"What is that big, white boat doing in the sky?" she asked herself. "I want to find out."

Find Text Evidence

Underline and read aloud the words *great* and *climb*.

Talk about the prediction you made about Fern. Correct it if you need to.

"It would be great to ride on that big white boat," Fern said. So she **stretched** her wings and took off.

Fern's wings helped her climb up, up, up.

But when she got close to the boat, she was surprised. The boat looked like a fluffy bed!

Find Text Evidence

Underline and read aloud the words *through* and *another*.

Talk about why Fern fell through the beds.

Fern was sleepy and wanted to rest.
So she **leaped** on the bed.
But she fell right through it!

"I see another bed," said Fern.
"I will try to land on that one."

But the same thing happened again!

"I'd better go home," cried Fern.
"Maybe Mom and Dad can
explain this."

Shared Read

 Find Text Evidence

Retell the story using the illustrations and words from the story.

Focus on Fluency

Take turns reading aloud to a partner.

- Read each word carefully.
- Read so it sounds like speech.

So Fern began to fly home. As she did, the beds turned dark gray. Then it started to rain. Poor Fern was soaked when she got home.

"Where were you?" asked Mom and Dad.

Fern told them all about her trip.

"First we will dry you off," said Mom.

"Then we will teach you about clouds," added Dad.

And that is what they did!

Vocabulary

 Listen to the sentences and look at the photos.

 Talk about the words.

 Write your own sentences using each word.

leaped

The frog **leaped** into the lake.

I leaped in water.

stretched

The rainbow **stretched** out across the sky.

I stretched my leg.

Think about small differences in meaning between words to better understand what you read.

Find Text Evidence

I know *great* and *good* have similar meanings, but *great* means "wonderful." I can tell that Fern thinks riding the boat would be more than just good!

"It would be great to ride on that big white boat," Fern said.

Your Turn

Think about the word *soaked* on page 50. What word do you know with just a small difference in meaning?

_____

_____

Remember, a **fantasy** is a story with made-up characters and events that could not happen in real life.

 Reread and think about the characters.

 Talk about what makes this a fantasy story. Think about the characters and events.

 Write how you know the story is a fantasy.

Characters and Events	Why It Could Not Happen In Real Life

Remember, a **cause** is what makes something happen in a story. An **effect** is the event that happens. All of the events together make up the **plot**.

 Reread "A Bird Named Fern."

 Talk about what happens and why it happens.

Write about the plot of the story by giving details about causes and effects.

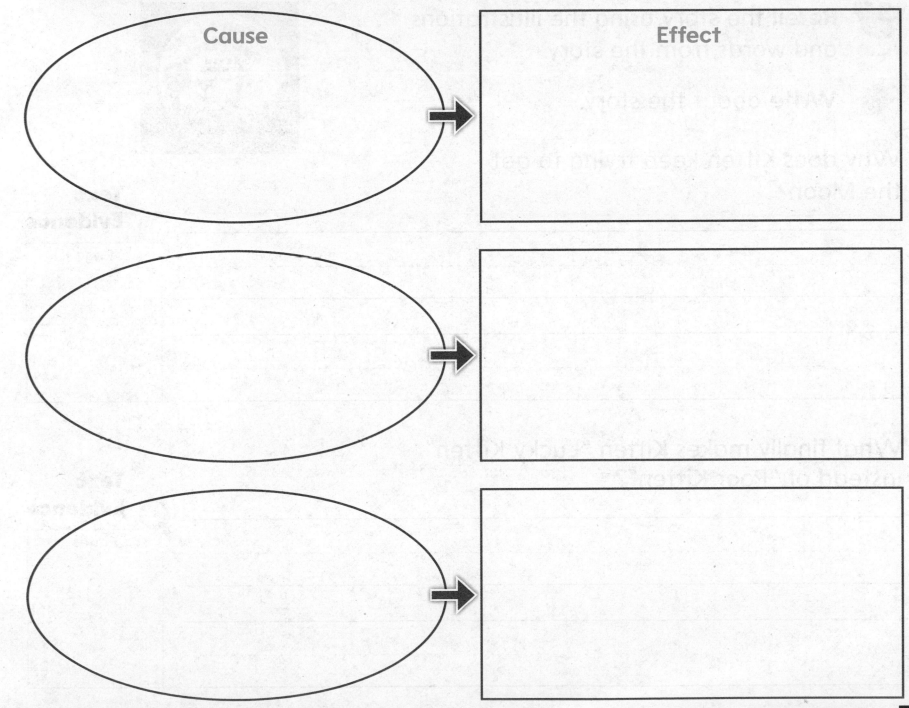

Cause

Effect

Retell the story using the illustrations and words from the story.

Write about the story.

Why does Kitten keep trying to get the Moon?

Text Evidence

Page

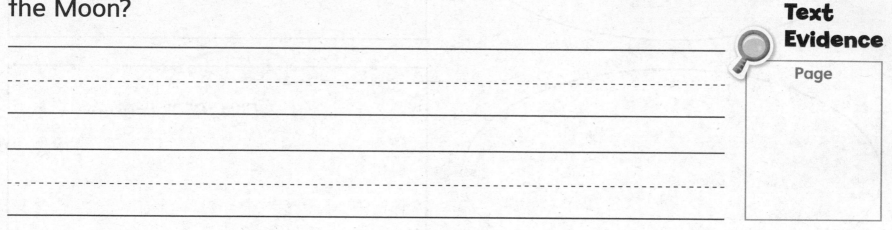

What finally makes Kitten "Lucky Kitten" instead of "Poor Kitten"?

Text Evidence

Pages

Talk about how Fern and Kitten are the same and different.

Write about Fern and Kitten.

What are Fern and Kitten both wrong about?

_____

- -

_____

- -

_____

Which character do you think is happier at the end of each story? Why?

_____

- -

_____

- -

_____

Focus on Fluency

Take turns reading aloud to a partner from *Kitten's First Full Moon.*

- Read each word carefully.

- Read so it sounds like speech.

- Read sentences with exclamation marks louder than other sentences.

Talk about what Kitten tries to do on pages 166 and 170.

Write about what Kitten tries to do to the Moon each time. Talk about this pattern.

First, Kitten tries . . .	Then, Kitten tries . . .

What is the author's purpose for using this pattern? Share your answer.

_____

- -

_____

_____

- -

Talk about the sentence that the author repeats on pages 168–169 and 172–173.

 Write the sentence. Then write what the sentence helps you visualize.

Repeated Sentence	What I Visualize

Why does the author repeat the sentence?
Share your answer.

_____

- -

_____

- -

_____

Talk about what Kitten sees on pages 180–181.

Write clues that show what Kitten thinks.

Text and Illustration Clues

⬇

Kitten thinks . . .

How do the text and illustration help you understand what is happening in the story? Share your ideas.

_____

_____

Write About It

Why couldn't Kitten drink the milk in the sky? How do you know?

The Moon

In 1902, young children thought that the Moon was made of cheese. Some saw the face of a man in the Moon.

Then telescopes helped us see the Moon better. The telescopes showed hills and flat places. They showed craters, or big holes, too.

We can see the Moon better with a telescope.

Read the title. Make a prediction about the text.

Underline what helped us see the Moon better.

Talk about how telescopes helped us learn more about the Moon.

Steve Cole/Photographer's Choice/Getty Images; (inset) somchaisom/iStock/360/Getty Images

Then, in 1961, astronauts went into space. In 1969, other astronauts walked on the Moon! They got a real close-up look.

Nothing grows on the Moon. It is very rocky. Astronauts brought back Moon rocks for us to see.

Maybe one day you will go to the Moon, too!

Astronauts went into space and landed on the Moon.

 Circle two details that describe the Moon.

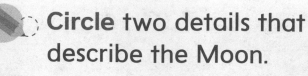 **Talk** about the caption. What does it help you understand?

 Talk about your prediction. Did the photo and caption change it? How?

Quick Tip

Use sentence starters to talk about the caption:

The caption tells . . . about . . .

I see . . .

NASA Headquarters - Greatest Images of NASA (NASA-HQ-GRIN)

Talk about what people used to think the Moon was made of.

 Write about what people thought about the Moon. Then write what they learned.

What People Thought About the Moon	Facts People Learned About the Moon

Why does the author tell what people once thought about the Moon? Share your answer.

_____

- -

_____

- -

_____

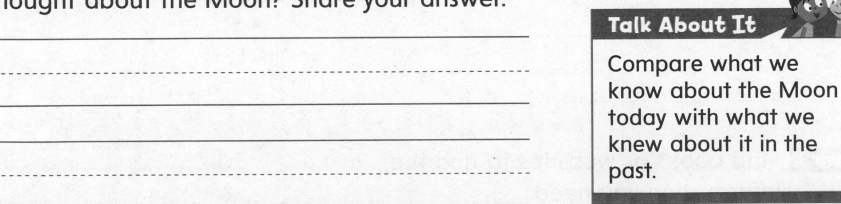

Talk About It

Compare what we know about the Moon today with what we knew about it in the past.

The Moon and Its Phases

Step 1 Use a print or online dictionary to find out the meaning of *phase*. Write the definition.

_____

- -

_____

Step 2 Write questions about the Moon's phases.

_____

- -

_____

- -

_____

- -

_____

Step 3 Find books or websites to find the information you need.

Step 4 Write the answers to your questions.

_____

- -

_____

_____

- -

_____

_____

- -

_____

Step 5 Draw and label what you learned about the phases of the Moon.

Step 6 Choose how to present your work.

Talk about what you see in this photo. Use complete sentences.

Compare how the sky in the photo is different from the sky in "The Moon."

Mario Eder/Moment/Getty Images

This person paraglides in the open sky above the mountains.

What I Know Now

Think about the texts you heard and read this week about the sky. Write what you learned.

_____

- -

_____

_____

- -

_____

_____

- -

_____

 Think about what else you would like to learn about the sky. Talk about your ideas.

 Share one thing you learned this week about fantasy stories.

Talk About It

Essential Question What inventions do you know about?

Talk about how you use this invention. Be sure to speak in full sentences.

Write how the early television in the photo is different from today's televisions. How is it the same?

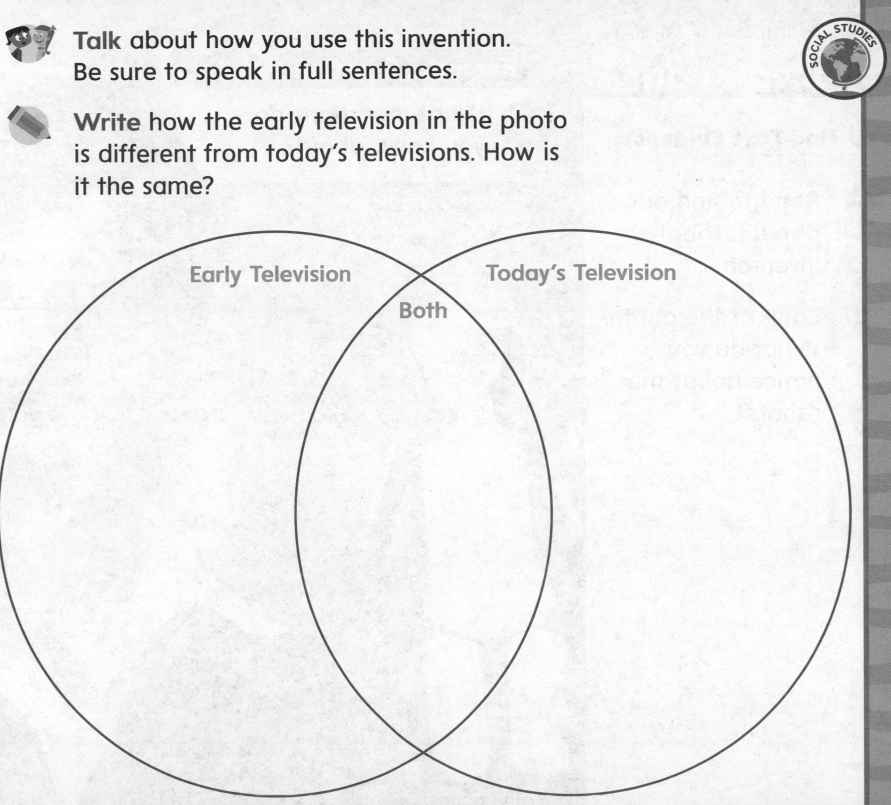

Early Television

Both

Today's Television

SuperStock

Shared Read

Find Text Evidence

Read to find out about a robot inventor.

Look at the photo. What do you notice about the robots?

Junko Kimura/Getty Images News/Getty Images

Essential Question

? What inventions do you know about?

The Story of a Robot Inventor

Shared Read

 Circle and read aloud the words with the *or* sound as in *for*.

Ask a question about the text. Read to find the answer to your question. Then tell the answer using full sentences.

Big Ideas

Meet Tomotaka Takahashi. He invents **unusual** robots. How did he get started?

Mr. Takahashi was born in Japan in 1975. As a child, he played with blocks. He used his imagination to make all sorts of forms and shapes.

Japan

Later, he read comic books about robots. One of the robots looked like a real child. Takahashi wanted to make robots just like it.

Find Text Evidence

Circle and read aloud the word spelled with *ore* as in *chore*.

Underline and read aloud the words *began, learn, right,* and *better*.

Finding Out About Robots

In 1999, Takahashi began to study robots. He took classes to learn how they move. The robots bent their legs when they walked. It did not look right to Takahashi. People did not walk that way.

Then Takahashi had an **idea**. He made a better robot. It did not bend its legs when it walked. It moved more like a person.

Koichi Kamoshida/Getty Images News/Getty Images

Shared Read

Find Text Evidence

Use clues from the text to figure out which robot is the strongest. Talk about your answer.

Talk about how you can tell Takahashi is good with robots.

Making Better Robots

In 2003, Takahashi started his own company. He made many robots. A short robot climbed up a cliff with a rope. A bigger robot lifted a car with its arms. Another robot rode a bike for 24 hours.

Takahashi began to put his robots in contests. He made three robots for a sports race in Hawaii in 2011. The first robot had to swim. The second robot had to ride a bike. The third robot had to run. The robots had to do these tasks for a week!

Toru Yamanaka/AFP/Getty Images

Shared Read

Find Text Evidence

Ask a question if you do not understand something. Reread to find the answers.

Retell the text so it makes sense.

Focus on Fluency

Take turns reading aloud to a partner.

- Read each word carefully.

- Read so it sounds like speech.

For the race, there were many problems to solve. Takahashi made the swimming robot waterproof. He gave it arms like fins to help it swim faster. Another robot was able to ride its bike for 100 miles without breaking. The third robot ran for 26 miles!

What will Takahashi invent next? Will his robots fly and soar? Will they be his finest? We can only guess. We must wait and see.

Tomotaka Takahashi is sure of one thing. His robots will do more and more!

Vocabulary

Listen to the sentences and look at the photos.

Talk about the words.

Write your own sentences using each word.

idea

New bulbs are a good **idea**!

My idea is to make a cake.

unusual

This new bike is **unusual**.

I have sea a unusual car.

If a word is new to you, look for parts you know to figure out the meaning.

Find Text Evidence

I'm not sure what *unusual* means, but I know that *usual* means "common." The prefix *un-* means "not." I think *unusual* means "not common."

He invents un/usual robots.

Your Turn

Write the parts in *unlike*. What does it mean?

_____

- -

_____

- -

_____

- -

_____

A **biography** is a story about a real person's life. It is written by another person.

 Reread to find out what makes this text a biography.

 Talk about how you know it is a biography.

 Write the clues from the text that show this is a biography.

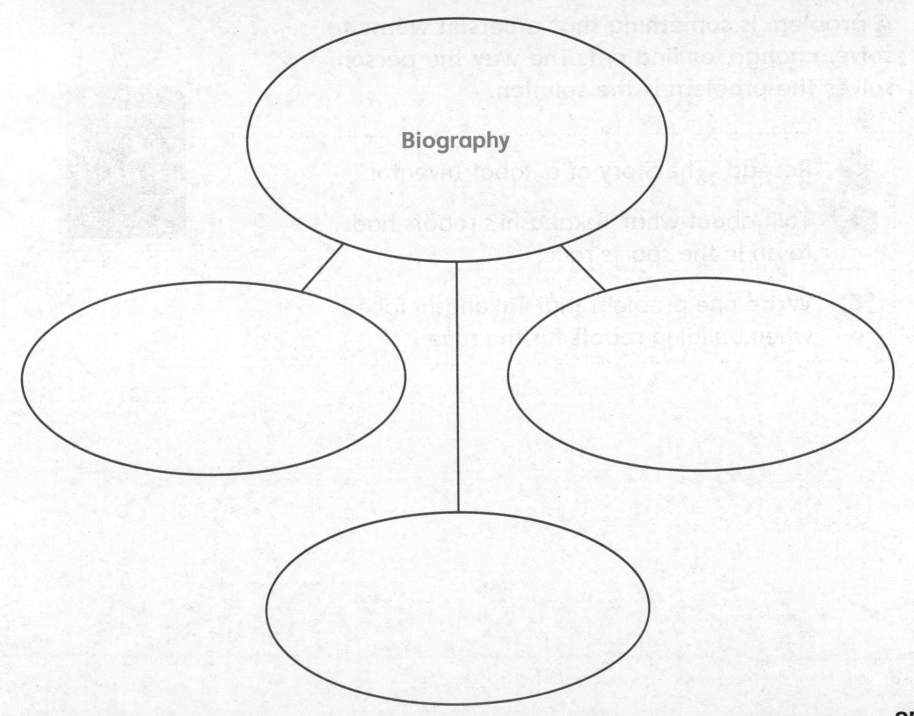

Biography

A **problem** is something that a person wants to solve, change, or find out. The way the person solves the problem is the **solution**.

 Reread "The Story of a Robot Inventor."

 Talk about what Takahashi's robots had to do in the sports race.

 Write one problem that Takahashi faced when building robots for the race.

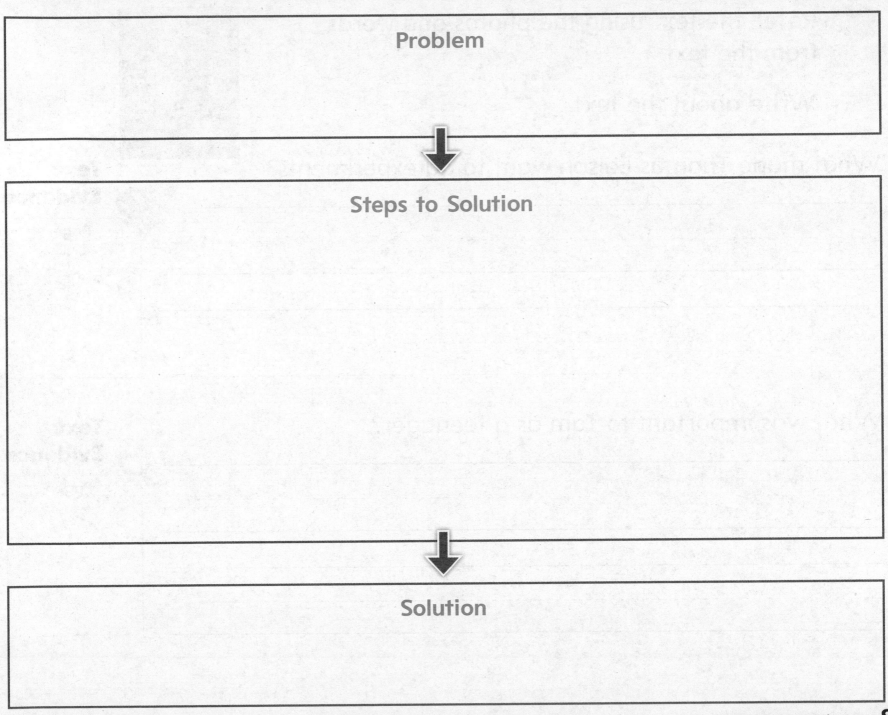

Problem

Steps to Solution

Solution

Retell the text using the photos and words from the text.

Write about the text.

Thomas Edison, Inventor

What made Thomas Edison want to do experiments?

_____

- -

_____

- -

_____

Text Evidence

Page

What was important to Tom as a teenager?

_____

- -

_____

- -

_____

Text Evidence

Page

Talk about how the texts are the same and different. Speak in complete sentences.

Write about the texts.

How are Tomotaka Takahashi and Thomas Edison alike?

_____

- -

_____

- -

_____

What do Tom's early experiments teach you about scientists?

_____

- -

_____

_____

- -

_____

Combine Information

Think about how your ideas about each scientist changed as you read.

First, I thought the scientist . . .

Then I thought . . .

Talk about what you learn about young
Tom on pages 204–207.

Write what young Tom wanted to know.
What did he do to find out about it?

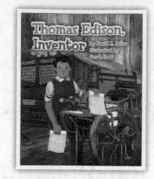

Tom wanted to know . . .	Tom experimented by . . .

Why does the author include stories about Tom
Edison when he was young? Share your ideas.

_____

_____

_____

Talk about what you learn about Tom on pages 210–214.

Write what Tom did and why.

What Tom Edison Did	Why He Did It

Why does the author include stories about Thomas Edison as he got older? Share your ideas.

_____

- -

_____

- -

_____

Talk about page 214. How did people send messages before there were telephones?

Write the steps Tom took that led him to invent new ways to use the telegraph.

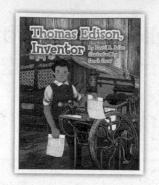

First	Next	Then

How does the author show that Tom kept trying new things? Share your answer.

_____

- -

_____

- -

_____

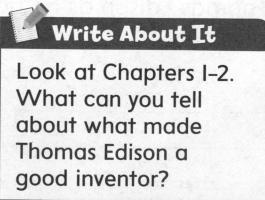

Write About It

Look at Chapters 1–2. What can you tell about what made Thomas Edison a good inventor?

Talk about the words the author repeats.

Write the repeated words. What do they tell you about windshield wipers?

Repeated Words	What They Tell About Windshield Wipers

Why does the author repeat the words?
Share your ideas.

_____

- -

_____

- -

_____

Great Inventions 93

Talk about what scissors look like.

Write what the author writes at the start and end of the poem to tell what X means.

Start	End

Why does the author start and end the poem with the letter *X*? Share your ideas.

_____

- -

_____

- -

_____

Quick Tip

Think about what you know about scissors.

Scissors look like . . .

When you open scissors, they . . .

Read aloud with a partner the words in the poems that begin with the same sounds.

Write the words with the same beginning sounds in each poem.

Windshield Wipers	Scissors

How do the words make the poem feel?

_____

- -

_____

_____

- -

_____

Write About It

Write your own poem about a great invention. Use repeating words or words that begin with the same sounds.

Research an Inventor

Step 1 **Choose** an inventor from this week to learn more about.

_____

- -

_____

Step 2 **Decide** what else you want to know about your inventor. Write your questions.

_____

- -

_____

- -

_____

- -

_____

Step 3 Find the information you need in books or
online. Read for answers to your questions.

Step 4 Write notes about your inventor.
Use a dictionary to look up
words to tell about your inventor.

_____

- -

_____

- -

_____

- -

_____

- -

_____

Step 5 Choose how to present your findings. You
may want to pretend to be your inventor
and tell the class about yourself.

Make Connections

 Talk about why this invention is a good idea.

 Compare the invention in the photo to the inventions Thomas Edison came up with to solve problems.

Mirrorpix/Newscom

Quick Tip

Explain about the invention using these sentence starters:

Some people need . . .

The invention helps . . .

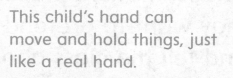

This child's hand can move and hold things, just like a real hand.

What I Know Now

Think about the texts you heard and read this week about inventions. Write what you learned.

_____

- -

_____

_____

- -

_____

_____

- -

_____

 Think about what else you would like to learn about inventions. Share your ideas.

 Share one thing you learned this week about biographies.

Talk About It

? **Essential Question** What sounds can you hear? How are they made?

Talk about how these children are making sounds. What are they using?

 Write the names of instruments. Then write sound words for each.

Instrument	Quiet or Loud?

Shared Read

Read

 Find Text Evidence

Think about the title and illustration. Ask a question about the story. Read on to find the answer.

Circle each word with the sound you hear in the middle of *found* and *down*.

Essential Question

? What sounds can you hear? How are they made?

Now, What's That Sound?

Realistic Fiction

Shared Read

Find Text Evidence

Underline and read aloud the words *early* and *thought*.

Ask a question about the sounds the kids hear. Read to find the answer.

Tap-tap-tap. Rat-a-tat-tat.

"What's that sound?" asked Gilbert. "It started early this morning. I thought it might stop, but it hasn't!"

"Let's check out the garage," said Marta. "I think Dad is making the sound."

Zing
Zing
Zing

Dad was in the garage cutting a board with his saw.

Zing, zing, zing.

"This is not the sound," said Gilbert. "This sound is smoother."

Find Text Evidence

Circle and read aloud each word on page 106 with the sound you hear in the middle of *found*.

Compare the sound Gramps is making to the sound the children are looking for.

"Let's find Gramps," said Marta. "He might be making the sound."

They quickly ran to the back of the house to find Gramps.

Gramps was sweeping the deck with a broom.

Swish, swish, swish.

"No, this is not the sound," said Gilbert. "This sound is much softer."

Swish
Wish
Swish

Find Text Evidence

 Underline and read aloud the word *instead*.

Talk about why Marta says "This is hopeless!"

"Let's find Ana instead," said Marta. "Maybe she's making the sound."

They found Ana in the driveway. Ana was bouncing a ball.

Bam. . . bam . . . bam.

Bam
Zing
Swish

"No, this is not the sound," said Gilbert. "This sound is slower."

"This is hopeless!" sighed Marta.

Find Text Evidence

 Ask any other questions you have. Reread to find the answers.

 Retell the story so it makes sense.

Focus on Fluency

Take turns reading aloud to a partner.

- Read each word carefully.

- Read so it sounds like speech.

Tap-tap-tap. Rat-a-tat-tat.

"There it is again," said Gilbert. He looked up at the tallest tree. **Suddenly**, he shouted. "Oh, wow! It's a bird!"

"Look at the color on its head," cried Marta. "It's red, like a red crown."

The bird **scrambled** up and down the tree.

Tap-tap-tap. Rat-a-tat-tat.

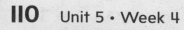

Tap-tap-tap!
Rat-a-tat-tat!

"It's a woodpecker pecking for bugs," said Gilbert.

"Yes," said Marta. "And nothing else sounds like it!"

Tap-tap-tap! Rat-a-tat-tat!

Vocabulary

 Listen to the sentences and look at the photos.

 Talk about the words.

 Write your own sentences using each word.

scrambled

Goats **scrambled** up the rocks.

_____

- -

_____

suddenly

The sky **suddenly** lit up brightly!

_____

- -

_____

If you don't know what a word means, look for word parts to help you figure out the meaning.

Find Text Evidence

I see the suffix -*less* at the end of the word *hopeless*. I can use the meaning of -*less* to figure out that *hopeless* means "without hope."

"This is hopeless!" sighed Marta.

Your Turn

Use what you know about the meaning of the suffix -*ly* to figure out the meaning of the word *quickly* on page 106.

_____

_____

_____

Realistic fiction is a made-up story that has characters, a setting, and events that can happen in real life. It has dialogue, or words that characters speak, that shows something about a character or adds story details.

 Reread to think about what makes this story realistic fiction.

 Talk about how you know it is realistic fiction.

 Write something you learn about the characters from the dialogue.

Character	What I Learned From the Dialogue

A **problem** is something characters want to solve, change, or find out. The way the problem is solved is the **solution**.

 Reread "Now, What's That Sound?"

 Talk about Gilbert and Marta's problem. Share how they try and finally solve the problem.

Write about the problem and its solution.

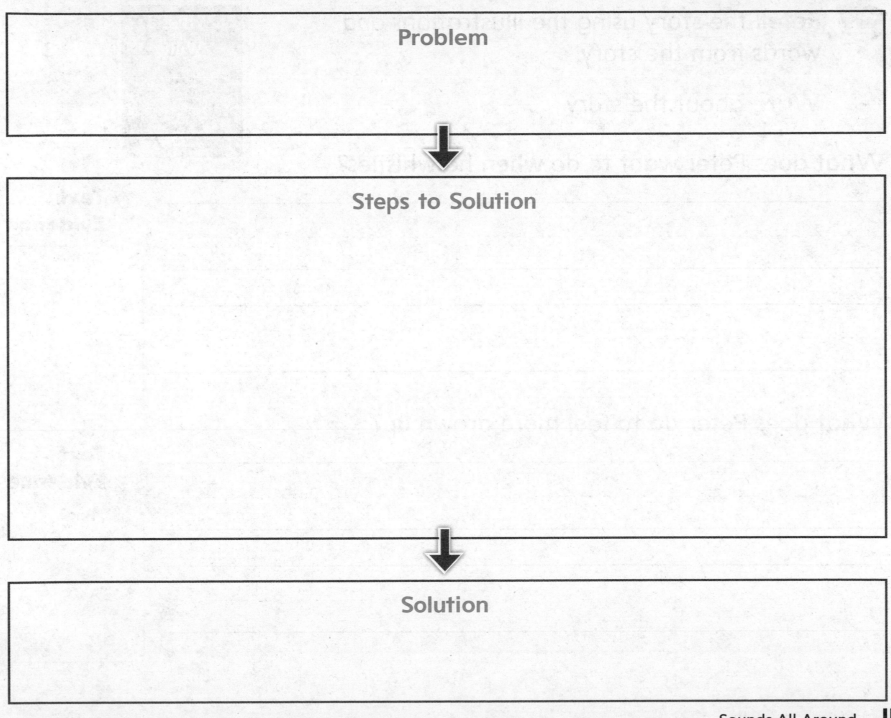

Problem

Steps to Solution

Solution

Retell the story using the illustrations and words from the story.

Write about the story.

Whistle for Willie
by Ezra Jack Keats

What does Peter want to do when he whistles?

_____

- -

_____

- -

_____

Text Evidence

Page

What does Peter do to feel more grown up?

_____

- -

_____

- -

_____

Text Evidence

Page

Talk about how the stories are the same and different.

 Write about the stories.

How is Gilbert and Marta's problem different from Peter's problem?

_____

_____

_____

How do you feel when you can solve a problem like the characters did?

_____

_____

_____

Quick Tip

Talk about the problems:

Gilbert and Marta want . . .
Peter wants . . .

Talk about what Peter is doing on pages 231–233.

 Write clues that help you know how Peter feels when he stops.

Illustration Clues	Story Clues

How does Peter feel? How does the author let you know how Peter feels? Share your answers.

_____

- -

_____

- -

_____

Talk about Peter's plan on pages 234–237. Why does he want to whistle?

 Write what happens on these pages.

Pages 234–235	Pages 236–237

How does the author help you know that Peter won't give up trying to whistle? Share your ideas.

_____

_____

_____

_____

👧👦 Talk about pages 246-248. What does Peter do before he whistles?

✏️ Write what each clue tells you about how Peter feels.

Whistle for Willie
by Ezra Jack Keats

Suddenly—out came a real whistle! ➡️ Peter feels...

"It's me," Peter shouted and stood up. ➡️ Peter feels...

How does the author help you know how Peter feels when he finally whistles? Share your ideas.

_____

- -

_____

- -

_____

Write About It

Use what you know about Peter to write a new story about a time he learned to play a musical instrument or to sing a special song.

Shake! Strike! Strum!

Make these instruments and start a band!

How to Make a Guitar

What You Need

- tissue box
- tape
- rubber bands
- ruler

What to Do

1. Stretch four to six rubber bands around the box.

2. Tape a ruler to the back. This is the guitar's neck.

3. Decorate the guitar.

4. Strum or pluck the rubber bands.

 Read to find out how to make instruments.

 Underline the first step when making a guitar.

 Talk about why the author uses numbers to show the steps.

How to Make a Shaker

What You Need

- plastic bottle

- dried beans

- stickers

What to Do

1. Put beans into a bottle.

2. Put fun stickers on it.

3. Shake and have fun.

Now you can shake, strike, strum, and have some fun!

Circle the materials in the "What You Need" list that are used in step one.

Underline what you should do after you decorate the bottle.

Talk about why the author wrote three steps.

Quick Tip

Use a sentence starter to talk about the steps:

The author wrote three steps because each step . . .

Talk about the sections of the text on page 124.

 Write what each section tells about.

"What You Need"	"What to Do"

Why did the author include both sections?

_____

- -

_____

- -

_____

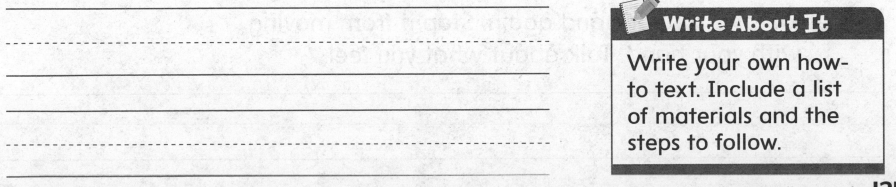

Write About It

Write your own how-to text. Include a list of materials and the steps to follow.

Rubber Band Sounds

Step 1 Put a rubber band across a bowl.

Step 2 Pull the rubber band and let go. Write what you see and hear.

_____

- -

_____

_____

- -

_____

_____

- -

_____

Step 3 Pull the rubber band again. Stop it from moving with your hand. Talk about what you feel.

_____

- -

_____

Step 4 **Write** what you think will change if you use rubber bands and bowls of different sizes.

_____

- -

_____

_____

- -

_____

Step 5 **Use** rubber bands and bowls of different sizes. Write the results.

_____

- -

_____

_____

- -

_____

Step 6 **Choose** how to present your findings. You may want to give a performance using your rubber bands and bowls.

Sing the song. Then talk about what part of the car is making the last sound in the song.

 Compare the sound words with the sound words you read in "Now, What's That Sound?"

I Have a Car

I have a car, it's made of tin.
Nobody knows what shape it's in.
It has four wheels and a rumble seat.
Hear us chugging down the street.
Honk honk
Rattle rattle rattle
Crash beep beep.

Dorling Kindersley/Vetta/Getty Images

What I Know Now

Think about the texts you heard and read this week about sounds. Write what you learned.

_____

_ _

_____

_ _

_____

_ _

_____

 Think about what else you would like to learn about sounds. Talk about your ideas.

 Share one thing you learned this week about realistic fiction.

Talk About It

Essential Question **How do things get built?**

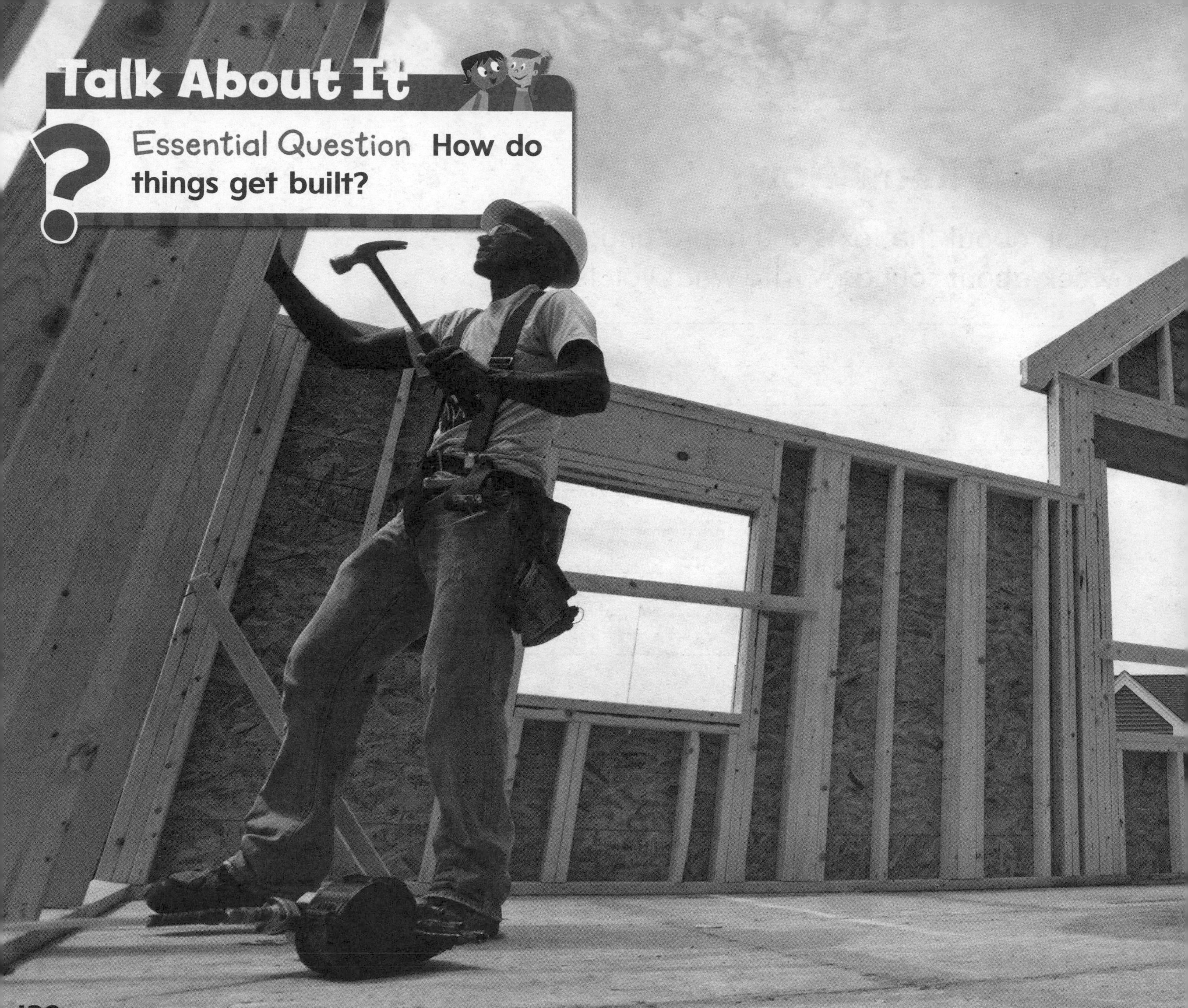

Talk and ask questions about what this carpenter is building. What is he using?

Write words about building things.

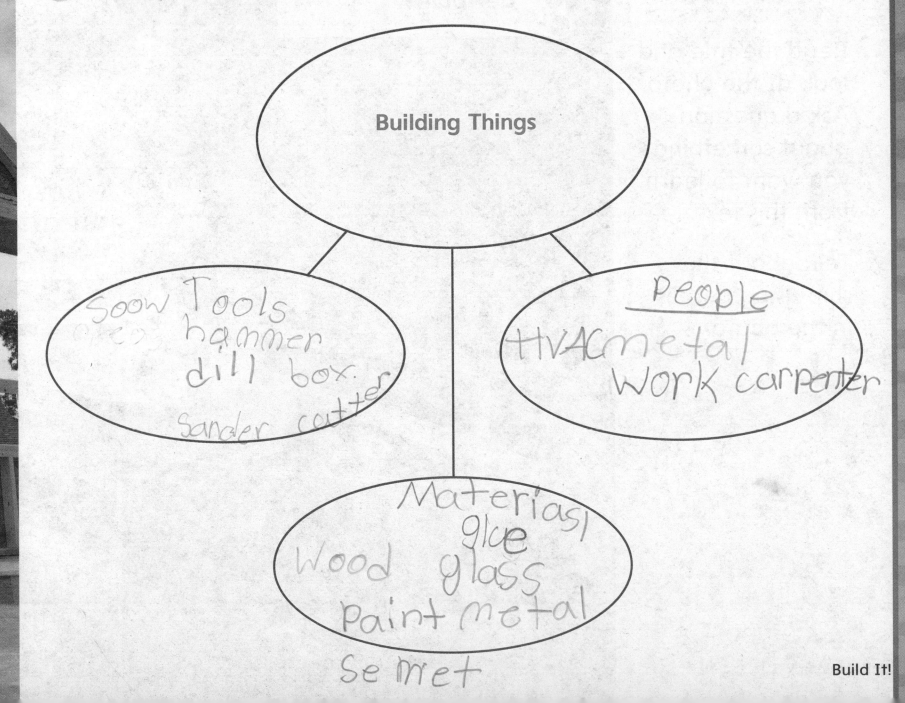

Building Things

Soow Tools
hammer
dill box.
sander cutter

People
HVACmetal
Work carpenter

Materiasl
glue
Wood glass
Paint metal
Se met

Huntstock/Getty Images

Shared Read

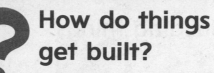

🔍 **Find Text Evidence**

Read the title and look at the photo. Ask a question about something you want to learn from this text.

Talk about the ship using details in the photo.

The Joy of a Ship

Ships take people and things all over the world. How does a ship get made? Find out here!

glass hall
A welle
metal
crane
W

Shared Read

🔍 **Find Text Evidence**

 Underline and read aloud the words *build, above,* and *fall.*

Circle and read aloud the word with the *oy* sound spelled *oy* as in *toys.*

What is needed to build a ship? Making ships employs many workers. This task uses lots of tools and parts as well. Let's see how a ship is made, step by step.

These people study the plans for the ship. There are many things to do!

Frame It!

First, workers build a frame. The ship frame can **balance** on blocks up above a dock. Huge cranes hoist the big parts in place so they do not fall. Workers must avoid being bumped by these big pieces of steel.

Some huge gantry cranes can lift 1,500 tons as high as 230 feet in the air.

Bogdan Wankowicz/Alamy

Sheets of Steel

Find Text Evidence

 Talk about details in the photos that help you understand the dangers of working with steel.

 Ask a question you have about the text so far. Read to find the answer.

First, two kinds of metal are melted into steel. It boils! Hot steel flows into flat metal sheets and molds. When steel gets cold, it gets hard. The steel sheets are then ready for making a ship.

Stand back! The steel is very hot!

A worker joins each steel **section**
by heating the edges, called joints.
Workers put on gloves and a helmet
to protect their hands and head.

enviromantic/Vetta/Getty Images

Check It, Paint It

Workers check all the joints. Then they point out leaks and fix them. If a joint leaks, the inside of this ship will be moist with water. It might even sink!

Fritz Hoffmann/The Image Works

Welder

Then, the ship is painted, and this job is done! It gleams in the sun. The workers knew it would look nice! People will pay a lot of money to ride on this ship.

Find Text Evidence

Ask any other questions you have. Reread to find the answers.

Retell the text so it makes sense.

Focus on Fluency

Take turns reading aloud to a partner.

- Read each word carefully.

- Read so it sounds like speech.

David Roark/Disney/Getty Images Entertainment/Getty Images

Out to Sea!

The people on the dock point with joy as the new ship begins the first trip! Those on the ship wave as it glides toward the open sea.

Did you know?

There are many kinds of ships on the sea.

Ice Breaker Ship ▼

Aircraft Carrier ▼

Cargo Ship ▼

Nonfiction

Vocabulary

Listen to the sentences and look at the photos.

Talk about the words.

Write your own sentences using each word.

balance

The worker can **balance** up high.

I can blance my Pen

section

This **section** is not finished yet.

Is section is not done.

Inflectional Endings

The -ed ending on an action word means the action happened in the past. To figure out the meaning of a word ending in -ed use the meaning of the root word and the ending.

🔍 Find Text Evidence

I can use the meaning of *melt* and *-ed* to figure out that *melted* means a solid became a liquid in the past.

First, two kinds of metal are melted into steel.

Your Turn

How can you figure out the meaning of *painted* on page 139? What does it mean?

_____

- -

_____

Remember, a **nonfiction** text gives facts about real things. It uses text and photos to give information.

 Reread to find information in the text and photos.

 Talk about the information.

 Write something you learn from the text and photos on pages 135 and 136.

Information from Text: Page 135	Information from Photo: Page 135

Information from Text: Page 136	Information from Photo: Page 136

A **cause** in a text is how or why something happens. An **effect** is what happens.

 Reread "The Joy of a Ship."

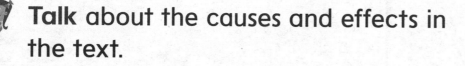 **Talk** about the causes and effects in the text.

 Write what causes hot steel to get hard. Then write about other causes and effects in the text.

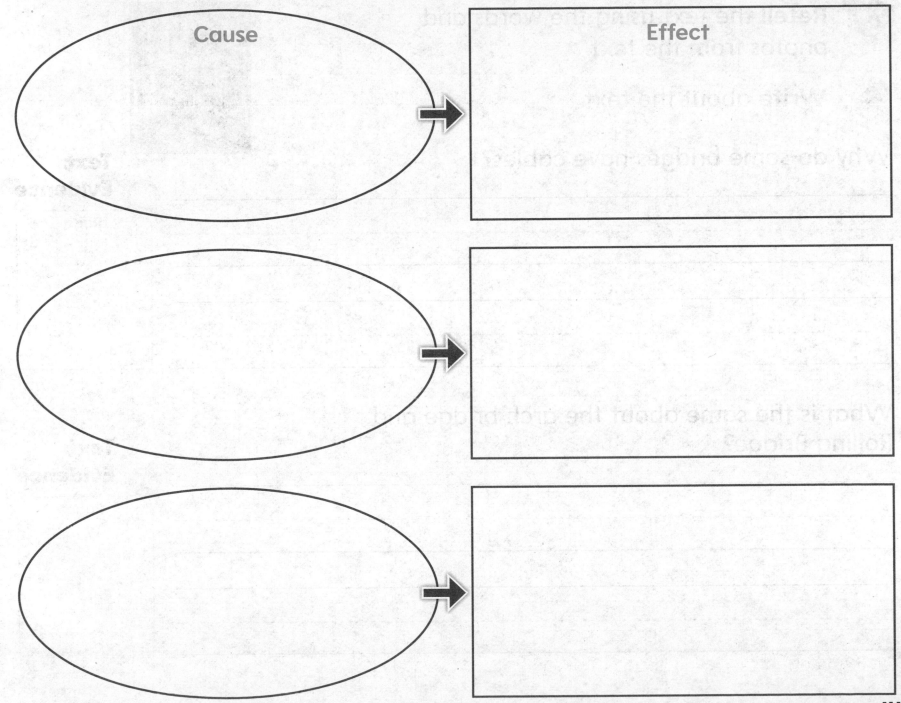

Cause

Effect

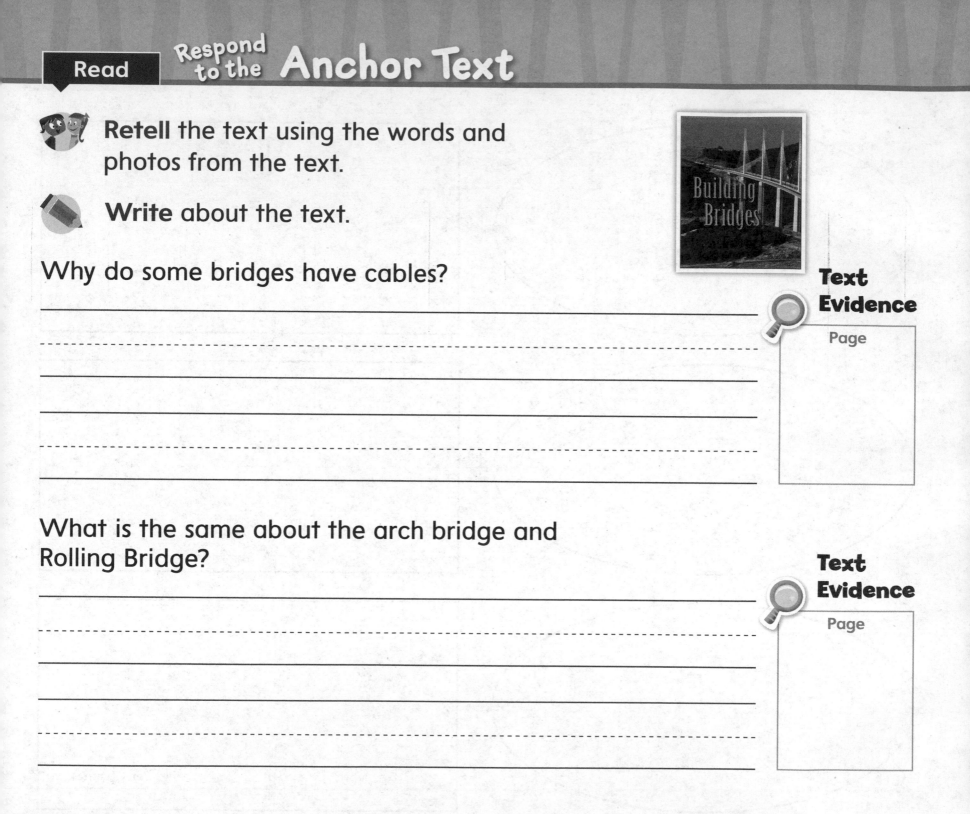

Retell the text using the words and photos from the text.

Write about the text.

Why do some bridges have cables?

_____

- -

_____

_____

- -

_____

Text Evidence

Page

What is the same about the arch bridge and Rolling Bridge?

_____

- -

_____

_____

- -

_____

Text Evidence

Page

Talk about how bridges and ships are the same and different.

 Write about bridges and ships.

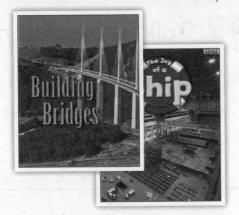

What kind of materials are used to build bridges and ships?

_____

_____

_____

How are the texts different?

_____

_____

_____

Make Inferences

Use clues to figure out things that are not stated.

Ships are made of steel. How are the materials for building bridges like steel?

Talk about the photos on pages 260–263.

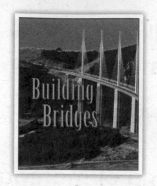

Write what you read in each caption.
Talk about what the captions tell you.

page 261	page 262	page 263

How does the author's use of captions help you
understand the text? Share your answer.

_____

_____

_____

_____

Talk about what the author asks on pages 264–266. Where can you find the answers?

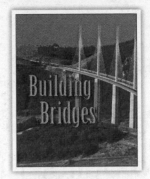 Use clues from the questions and answers to write what makes each bridge special.

Firth of Forth Bridge	Golden Gate Bridge	Rolling Bridge

Why does the author ask and answer questions in the text? Share your answer.

_____

- -

_____

- -

_____

Write About It

Which bridge do you think is the most interesting? Why?

Small Joy

Tiny houses do not take a long time to build. Tiny houses do not cost a lot. And tiny houses do not take a lot of energy or materials. They are good for the earth!

Tiny houses can go where their owners go!

Read to find out why tiny houses are good things.

Underline three things that are good about tiny houses.

Talk about how the author feels about tiny houses.

Quick Tip

Look at punctuation marks for a clue to the author's feelings.

Dee Williams

Talk about what "joy" means.

 Write clues from the text and photos that tell about tiny houses.

Clues in the Text	Clues in the Photos

Why did the author name this text "Small Joy?" Share your answer.

_____

- -

_____

- -

_____

Talk About It

How do the text, photos, and captions help you understand why people build tiny houses?

How to Build a(n) _____

Step 1 Choose something you want to learn how to build using materials found in nature.

_____

- -

_____

Step 2 Write questions about building your item.

_____

- -

_____

- -

_____

- -

_____

Step 3 Find the information you need in books or online.

Step 4 **Write** what you learned about how to build your item. Use a dictionary to find and spell words about the materials you can use.

Materials	Steps to Build a(n) _____

Step 5 **Choose** how to present your work.

Tell what you learn about the U.S. Capitol building from the photo and caption.

 Compare what you read about building a bridge to building the Capitol.

Quick Tip

Compare using these sentence starters:

Building a bridge . . .

Building the Capitol also . . .

It took a lot of years, money, and people to build the U.S. Capitol building. People do important work for our government there.

What I Know Now

Think about the texts you heard and read about building things. Write what you learned.

_____

- - - - - - - - - - - - - - - - - - - -

_____

- - - - - - - - - - - - - - - - - - - -

_____

- - - - - - - - - - - - - - - - - - - -

_____

- - - - - - - - - - - - - - - - - - - -

_____

 Talk about what else you would like to learn about building things.

 Share one thing you learned this week about nonfiction texts.

Writing and Grammar

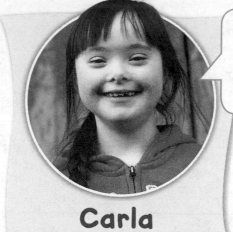

Carla

I wrote a how-to text to teach others how to make a target game.

Student Model

How to Make a Target Game

What You Need

tape that is sticky on both sides

four table tennis balls

three sheets of felt in different colors

scissors

glue

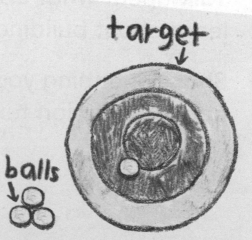

target

balls

How-To Text

My how-to text gives the steps for making something.

What to Do

1. Cover the balls with the tape.

2. Cut out three felt circles. Make a large one, a medium one, and a small one.

3. Stack and glue the felt circles from largest to smallest.

4. Hang the target on a wall. Throw a ball and watch it stick to the target!

Genre

 Talk about what makes Carla's text a how-to text.

 Ask any questions you have about how-to texts.

 Circle the third step for how to make a target game.

Plan

 Talk about ideas for your how-to text.

Draw or write about the ideas.

Choose something to write a how-to text about.

_____

- -

_____

Describe what your how-to text will teach
others to do. Think about the steps.

_____

- -

_____

- -

_____

- -

_____

- -

_____

Writing and Grammar

Draft

Read Carla's draft of her how-to text.

Organization

All of the details I wrote tell about making a target game.

Student Model

How to Make a Target Game

What You Need

tape that is sticky on both sides

four table tennis balls

felt in different colors

scissors

glue

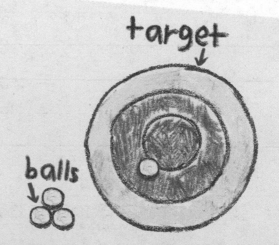

target

balls

What to Do

1. Cover the balls with the tape.

2. Cut out three felt circles. Make a large one, a medium one, and a small one.

3. Stack and glue the felt circles from largest to smallest.

4. Hang the target. Throw a ball and watch it stick to the target!

Sequence

The steps in my how-to text are in sequence.

Your Turn

Begin to write your how-to text in your writer's notebook. Use your ideas from pages 160–161. Be sure all your details tell about your idea.

Writing and Grammar

Revise and Edit

Think about how Carla revised and edited her how-to text.

I added details to give more information.

Student Model

How to Make a Target Game

What You Need

tape that is sticky on both sides

four table tennis balls

I spelled high frequency words correctly.

A three sheets of felt in different colors

scissors

glue

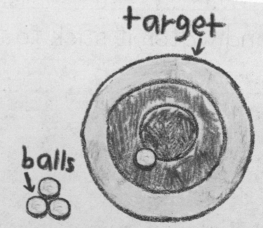

target

balls

Grammar

- Use *and, but,* and *or* to join sentences.
- Adjectives describe or compare nouns.
- Use the articles *a, an, this,* and *that* before nouns.
- Prepositions and prepositional phrases tell about nouns.

I made sure to use articles correctly.

What to Do

1. Cover the balls with the tape.

2. Cut out three felt circles. Make a large one, a medium one, and a small one.

3. Stack and glue the felt circles from largest to smallest.

4. Hang the target on a wall. Throw a ball and watch it stick to the target!

I added a preposition and a noun to tell where to hang the target.

Your Turn

Revise and edit your writing. Be sure to use joining words, adjectives, articles, and prepositions correctly.

Publish

 Finish editing your writing. Make sure it is neat and ready to publish.

 Practice presenting your work with a partner. Use this checklist.

 Present your work.

Review Your Work	Yes	No
Writing		
I wrote a how-to text.	☐	☐
I focused on one idea.	☐	☐
Speaking and Listening		
I listened carefully to my classmates.	☐	☐
I spoke when it was my turn.	☐	☐
I answered questions in complete sentences.	☐	☐

Talk with a partner about what you did well in your writing.

Write about your work.

What did you do well in your writing?

_____

- - - - - - - - - - - - - - - -

_____

- - - - - - - - - - - - - - - -

_____

What do you need to work on?

_____

- - - - - - - - - - - - - - - -

_____

- - - - - - - - - - - - - - - -

_____

Spiral Review

Genre:
- Fantasy
- How-To Text

Strategy:
- Make and Confirm Predictions, Ask and Answer Questions

Skill:
- Problem and Solution, Cause and Effect

Vocabulary Strategy:
- Suffixes, Prefixes

Look at the illustrations and read the title. Make a prediction about the story before you read it.

Shelly Goes Fast!

Shelly was late for school. Again. Her pals waved at her to go faster. But Shelly was just slow.

Shelly asked her pals for help. "How do you go fast?"
"I flutter," Carmen said.
"I scamper," Charlie said.
"I slither," Sid said.
Shelly tried to flutter, scamper, and slither.

But she still went slow.

As Shelly went home, she started thinking. Soon, she had a plan.

The next day, Shelly was the first at school.

"How did you get here so fast?" her pals asked.

"With this!" she cried, proudly showing them the skate she had made. "I can't flutter, scamper, or slither, but I can roll!"

At last, Shelly was not late.

Show What You Learned

Circle the correct answer to each question.

1 How can you tell the story is a fantasy?

A Turtles move slowly.

B Turtles do not speak.

C Turtles have shells.

2 The word *proudly* in the story means _____.

A without pride

B in a way that shows pride

C with very little pride

> **Quick Tip**
>
> Think about the parts in a word to figure out its meaning.

3 Shelly's problem is _____.

A she cannot move quickly.

B she's in trouble for being late.

C she doesn't know how to skate.

Read the text. Ask questions as you read. Then read on to find the answers.

How to Make Homemade Bubbles

What You Need

- one cup of dish soap
- six cups of water
- a bottle with a cap
- one-quarter cup of light corn syrup

Corn Syrup
16 FL. OZ. (1 PT.) .47L

Show What You Learned

What to Do

1. Uncap the bottle and fill it with the water.

2. Add the dish soap.

3. Add in the light corn syrup.

4. Put the cap on the bottle.

5. Let it sit overnight. This helps make the bubbles thicker, so they last longer.

6. Blow bubbles!

Bend pipe cleaners into fun shapes. Dip the ends into the bubble mix and blow!

🖉 **Circle** the correct answer to each question.

1 Why did the author write this text?

    A to teach important facts about bubbles
    B to show what bubbles look like
    C to tell how to make bubbles at home

2 Letting the bubble mix rest before using it causes the bubbles to _____.

    A last longer
    B smell better
    C be more colorful

3 The word *uncap* in the text means _____.

    A take off the cap
    B put the cap on again
    C twist the cap tight

Quick Tip

A cause can have more than one effect.

Focus on How-To Texts

A **how-to text** tells or teaches how to do something. It may have steps in a process.

 Reread "How to Make Homemade Bubbles" on pages 171–172.

 Talk about the sections of the text and what they tell about.

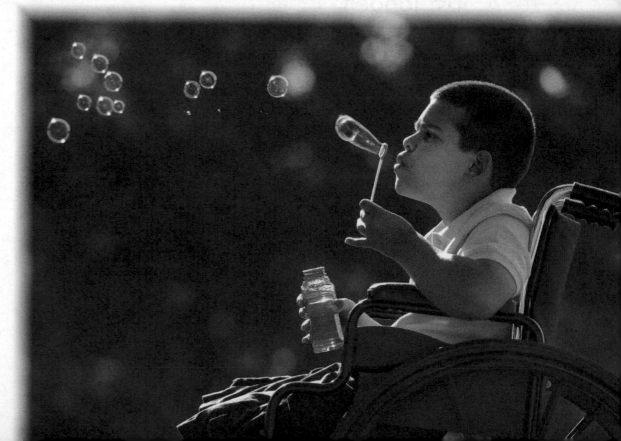

Write what kind of information the author gives in each section of the text.

"What You Need" Section	"What to Do" Section

Why does the author include both sections?
Share your answer.

_____

- -

_____

- -

_____

- -

_____

Extend Your Learning

Respond to the Read Aloud

A **problem** is something characters want to solve, change, or find out. The way the problem is solved is the **solution**.

 Listen to "Chen the Tapper."

Talk about Chen's problem and how he solves it.

Write about the problem and solution to Chen's problem.

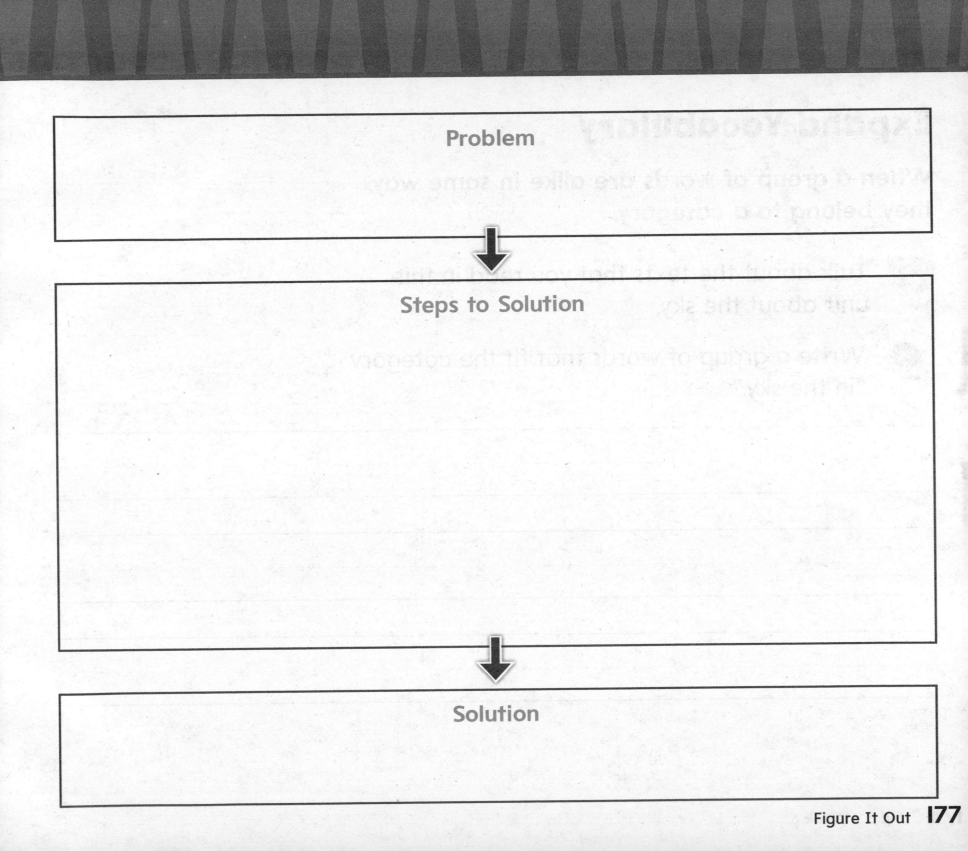

Problem

Steps to Solution

Solution

Expand Vocabulary

When a group of words are alike in some way, they belong to a **category**.

Talk about the texts that you read in this unit about the sky.

Write a group of words that fit the category "in the sky."

_____

_____

_____

_____

Talk about how the pictures in the chart are alike.

Write words that tell about each group.

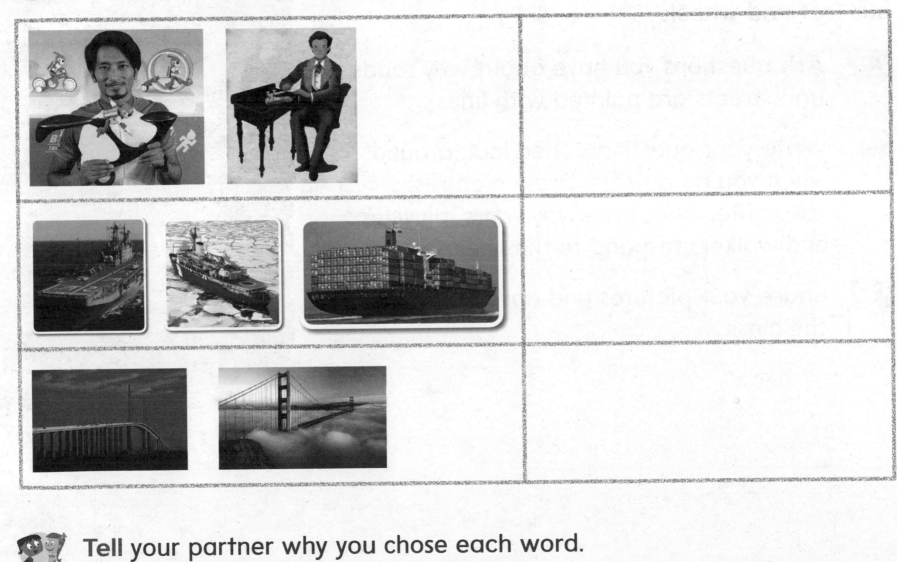

 Tell your partner why you chose each word.

Extend Your Learning

How Roads and Streets Work

You have thought about what is up in the sky. Now it's time to think about the ground beneath our feet and wheels.

 Ask questions you have about why roads and streets are painted with lines.

 Write your questions. Then look around when you go outside. Draw pictures. Take notes about the ways cars, bicycles, and walkers respond to the lines.

 Share your pictures and answers with the class.

Reading Digitally TIME FOR KIDS.

Sidebar features in online texts give more information about a topic.

Listen to "Great Ideas!" at my.mheducation.com. Then click on the sidebar features.

Talk about the sidebar features.

Write about the information in "Cool Inventions" and "Which Came First?"

_____
- -
_____
- -
_____
- -
_____
- -
_____
- -
_____

Write a How-To Text

You can teach or tell others how to do something by writing a **how-to text**.

 Reread "Shake! Strike! Strum!" and "How to Make Homemade Bubbles."

 Talk about how the texts are alike.

 List the parts in a how-to text. Write what information each part gives.

_____

_____

_____

_____

_____

_____

_____

Talk about something you know how to do or make.

 Write a how-to text. Be sure to include all the steps.

Choose Your Own Book

 Tell a partner about a book you want to read. Say why you want to read it.

Quick Tip

Try to read a little longer each time you read.

 Write the title.

_____

- -

_____

 Write about your opinion of the book you read. Give reasons for your opinion.

Minutes I Read

_____

- -

_____

- -

_____

- -

_____

What Did You Learn?

Think about the skills you have learned.
How happy are you with what you can do?

I understand cause and effect.	😊	😐	☹️
I understand problem and solution.	😊	😐	☹️
I use context clues to understand words with multiple meanings.	😊	😐	☹️
I can figure out the meaning of words with -ed and -ing endings.	😊	😐	☹️

What is something that you want to get better at?

_____

_____

_____

My Sound-Spellings

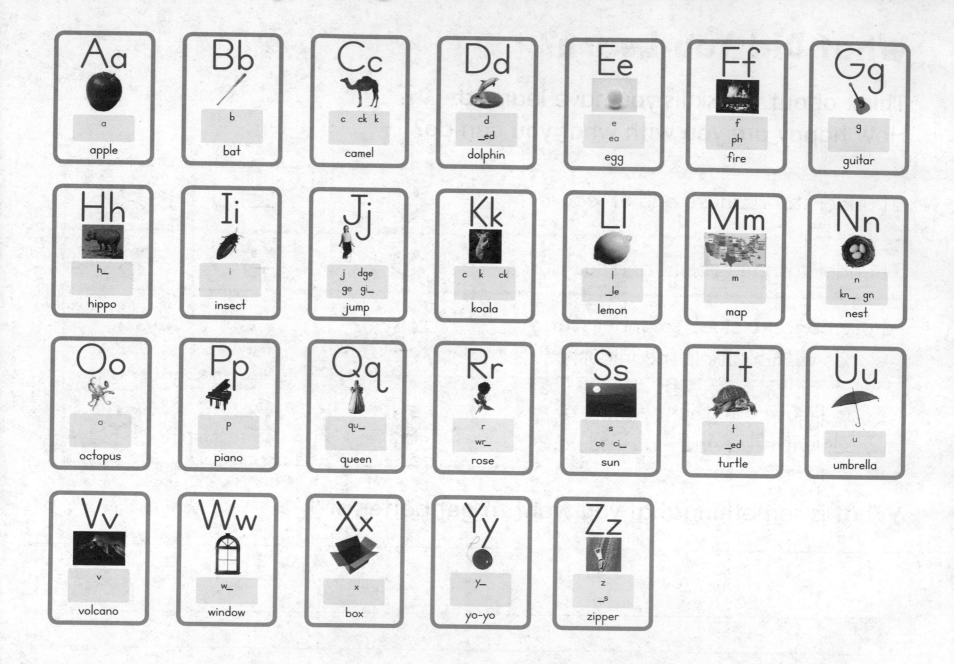

Aa apple
a

Bb bat
b

Cc camel
c ck k

Dd dolphin
d
_ed

Ee egg
e
ea

Ff fire
f
ph

Gg guitar
g

Hh hippo
h_

Ii insect
i

Jj jump
j dge
ge gi_

Kk koala
c k ck

Ll lemon
l
_le

Mm map
m

Nn nest
n
kn_ gn

Oo octopus
o

Pp piano
p

Qq queen
qu_

Rr rose
r
wr_

Ss sun
s
ce ci_

Tt turtle
t
_ed

Uu umbrella
u

Vv volcano
v

Ww window
w_

Xx box
x

Yy yo-yo
y_

Zz zipper
z
_s

Credits: (apple) Stockdisc/PunchStock; (bat) Radlund & Associates/Artville/Getty Images; (camel) Photodisc/Getty Images; (dolphin) imagebroker/Alamy; (egg) Pixtal/age fotostock; (fire) Comstock Images/Alamy; (guitar) Jules Frazier/Getty Images; (hippo) Michele Burgess/Corbis; (insect) Photodisc/Getty Images; (jump) Rubberball Productions/Getty Images; (koala) Al Franklin/Corbis; (lemon) C Squared Studios/Getty Images; (map) McGraw-Hill Education; (nest) Siede Preis/Photodisc/Getty Images; (octopus) Photographers Choice RF/SuperStock; (piano) Photo Spin/Getty Images; (queen) Joshua Ets-Hokin/Photodisc/Getty Images; (rose) Steve Cole/Photodisc/Getty Images; (sun) 97/E+/Getty Images; (turtle) Ingram Publishing/Fotosearch; (umbrella) Stockbyte/PunchStock; (volcano) Westend61/Getty Images; (window) Photodisc/Getty Images; (box) C Squared Studios/Getty Images; (yo-yo) D. Hurst/Alamy; (zipper) ImageState/Alamy

th	sh	ch tch	wh_	ng	a ai_ _ay a_e ea ei	i y i_e igh ie
thumb	shell	cheese	whale	sing	train	five

o oa ow o_e _oe	u u_e _ew _ue	e_e ea ee e _y ie _ey	ar	er ir ur or	oar or ore	ow ou
boat	cube	tree	star	shirt	corn	cow

oi _oy	oo	oo u_e u _ew ue ou ui	a aw au augh al	air are ear ere
boy	book	spoon	straw	chair

Handwriting Models

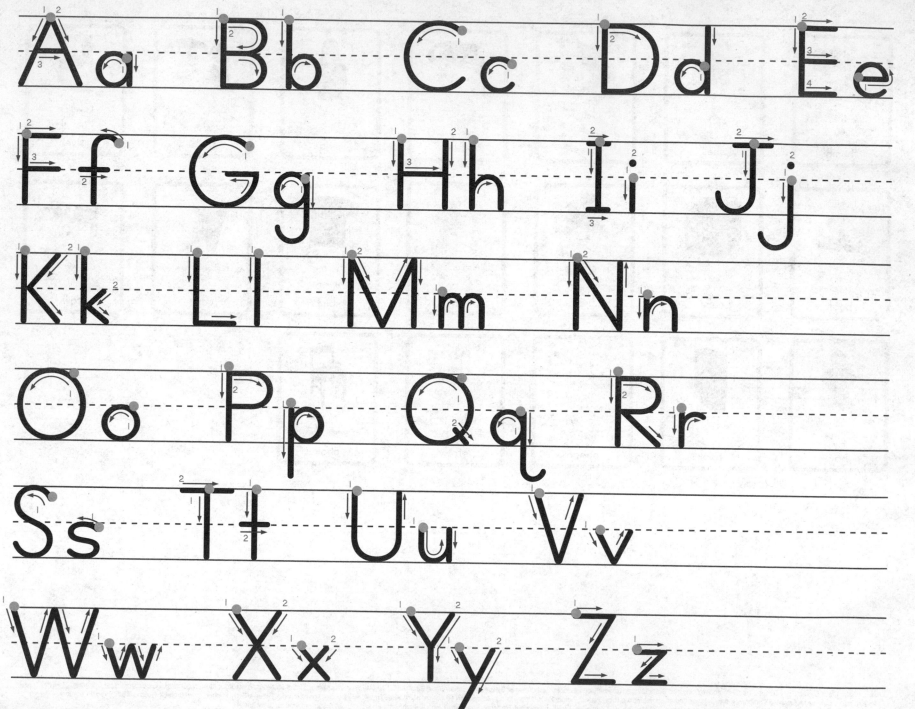